LIFE'S
Poetry

Be Inspired! Feel Inspired!
Stay Inspired!
This is your time...
Just Shine!

Josephine

LIFE'S
Poetry

Josephine Dion Casey

Library of Congress Control Number: 2013900736
ISBN: Hardcover   978-1-4797-7867-6
               Softcover   978-1-4797-7866-9
               Ebook   978-1-4797-7868-3

This book was printed in the United States of America.

For comments and / or inquiries, please feel free to contact the author by email at josephines.poetry@gmail.com

To order additional copies of this book, contact:
Xlibris Corporation
1-888-795-4274
www.Xlibris.com
Orders@Xlibris.com
126345

Contents

Life's Poetry

Some days are good
Some days are bad
Some days it's just enough you've had
Life's a mystery
Painting its history
Waiting to unfold
A story to be told
A way of living with elevated expressions of thought
That's life poetry
Life's poetry sought
Life is what we see and make it to be
The slightest opinions we think and feel
It can be overwhelming
Confusing and loosing
But it can be pleasing and uplifting
Always shifting
Life's a poetry in its own form
With ups and downs, winds and storms
It's how you overcome and supersede these times
That will truly be the test for you to shine
See life's poetry as an art you frame
Everyday something new
Or maybe the same
It's a view, a take on life too
Depends on what you intend to do
So strive for you
Hurt, pain
Power, fame

It's all apart of our human heart
The challenges and journeys through life
Help form and compose who you are
Different experiences
Different appearances
Some have it easy, some not
Some caught, some fought
It can also be how you process your thought
That again is life's poetry
Life's poetry sought

Inspired Again

I've been feeling inspired again
So inspired to tie up loose ends
So inspired to make things mend
Could this be a God-send
To start writing again
I've been inspired again

Acceptance With Open Arms

Accept me for who I am
I'm doing the best I can
Leaning closer to God at my pace
Yes I know I should hurry before it's too late
I don't want to be judged or looked upon with disgrace
So please just accept me for who I am
At this very moment, at this very place
My faith may not be as strong and firm as yours
But please do not treat me any differently because of this
I do believe in God and look forward to building on my faith
Yes I know I need to do this now before it's too late
So this is something you can help me embrace
Accept me for who I am with open arms you see
For only God alone can judge me and only he

It's A New Year

It's a new year
Start with no fear
A fresh start
Have more of a heart
Begin again
Time to mend
Leave the past
No more being last
Dream big
Take chances and dig
Find the happiness you need
In order to succeed
Change for the better
Share, love and care
It's a new year

Motivation

Motivation, concentration
Feel the power of this salvation
Striving always to do your best
Succeeding at the impossible test
Showing ambition
When obstacles arise on difficult missions
That's a tremendous decision
Doubts, fears, weary, tiredness
This is what some may confess
As the journey prolongs some think less
But stay focused
Redeem that attention
No need for contemplation
Just motivate, stimulate, innervate
Stay strong despite the worst of situations
Show that intuition
Acknowledge that inspiration
Unleash that exaltation
For it's your motivation

Reality Bites

Facing reality
Seeing the different faces
Different races
With different cases
They say reality bites
Sometimes we fail to see the lights
People battle problems
People have fights
Yes reality bites
This life has up's and downs
Everywhere in every town
Cities, countries, places
Everyone tells a story on their faces
Yes reality bites
So hold on, hold tight
Don't give up this fight
Reality bites

Pray And Don't Worry

Pray and don't worry
But we always seem
To be in a hurry
To have things right
And never out of sight
God has a plan for us
So take a seat and don't fuss
Pray and don't worry
Stop being in such a hurry
Yes this can be draining
And goes without saying
But pray and don't worry
And stop being in such a hurry

JOSEPHINE DION CASEY

Simplicity

Sometimes it's the simple things in life
That are to be cherished
They may not be the most expensive
Lavishing or fairest
Sometimes a simple life is all we need
For us to succeed
To be who we want to be
And take the lead
Sometimes a simple kind gesture
Is what people look for
Nothing less, nothing more
So open the door
Feel the galore
To simplicity

Forget My Fears That Has Brought Me To Tears

Lord give me strength to face today
Forget my fears
That has brought me to tears
Open my eyes to see the light
That will shine so bright
Shine on me
So I can be
Full of joy and grace again
Never failing to descend
Forget my fears
That has brought me to tears
I know someone out there cares
Lord this is you
I call your name
Keep me humble
Keep me safe
So I may forget my fears
That has brought me to tears

JOSEPHINE DION CASEY

I Can Do It

These thoughts I think of from time to time
Only God knows what's on my mind
Pushing these thoughts of negativity
Searching for the positivity
Using all my creativity
To show my best efforts and ability
I can do it I know I can
Sometimes I just need a helping hand
But these thoughts I think of from time to time
Only God knows there on my mind
He will help me push away the negativity
So I can see all the positivity
That shows my creativity
At my best ability
Because I can do it I know I can
With God's helping hand

Not Just A Pretty Face

A pretty face
Is that all you see
Over there looking at me
I have feelings
I have meanings
I'm not just a pretty face
Look on the inside
Instead of the outside
I am true and real
As I can ever be
See me for who I am
Try to understand
I'm not just a pretty face
Don't just sit there and miscalculate
Don't just sit there and underestimate
I have a set mind
A set state
I'm not just a pretty face
Can you relate
I have goals
I am ambitious
Not fake, not fictitious
Have fate
I'm not just a pretty face

JOSEPHINE DION CASEY

Where Are You Lord

Everyday struggles
Life seems so hard
Where are you Lord
I need you now
And I don't know what to do
And how
How to believe you will make things right
And be my shining light
Where are you Lord
I feel at such a loss
I need you now
Please show me how
How to believe in you again
And how you are a dear friend
Where are you Lord
Please help me see
See that you are here for me
Where are you Lord
Where are you

She Wears The Expression On Her Face

Happy sad
Cheerful glad
She wears the expression on her face
To crack a smile
Would be a while
She wears the expression on her face
Her eyes tell it all
Will she stand
Will she fall
She wears the expression on her face
Her body language sets it out
Is she thinking, does she have doubts
Can we tell by these words coming from her mouth
Or is it because
She wears the expression on her face

JOSEPHINE DION CASEY

Capture The Moment

Capturing these moments
Filled with joy, happiness, love and laughter
To remember now, tomorrow and after
Remembering the good times
Focusing on my mind
These moments of glee, exuberance and contentment
Oh such delight
And fulfillment these moments are
As I think on them to get me far
Ahead in life
Achieving success
And doing my utmost best
Nothing more, nothing less
For capturing these moments will carry me through
In life and in what I do

She's Only A Reflection Of Me

Why does she act that way
Is it because of me
Is it because of what I say
Shall I even say such things
Shall I dare
But could she be a reflection of me
Is this what I'm failing to see
Why does she have that look on her face
Could it be she's drank something that had a bad taste
Or could this be another reflection of me
Which again I fail to see
As I ask myself why so much struggles with her
Such a battle at times
Could it be something overwhelming her mind
Or again a missed sign that I fail to see
Because she's only a reflection of me

JOSEPHINE DION CASEY

I Am Strong

I am strong
In this I am not wrong
I am ambitious
And not fictitious
I keep things real
And this is how I feel
I am strong
I am motivated
Calm and sedative
I am peaceful
And not deceitful
I am strong
I am caring
Kind-hearted and sharing
And not fearing
For I am strong

Perception

Looking at you
I can see right through
A story you can tell
Of how you made it
And how you fell
Is this what I see
On your face misery
Or is it my view
My perception of you
Could I be right
Could I be wrong
Is this vision a speculation
Of what I perceive
You to be

It Can Be Such A Burden At Times

It can be such a burden at times
To constantly think and have wondrous minds
Thinking too much
Yes it's a human touch
Human touch that can cause us to act on impulses
Impulses so strong that we tend to forget what's right and wrong
This can be such a burden at times
That causes us to constantly think and have wondrous minds
Confusion may arise
And indecisive decisions
Can take over our minds with the wrong vision
See this can be such a burden at times
To constantly think and have wondrous minds

Patiently Waiting

Always patiently waiting
Never really hating
But when will it be my turn
I've been through a lot and have learned
Learned to persevere
Learned to stay silent and hear
Hear of others that are more in need
And always lending a hand and doing a good deed
So when will the good be rewarded for patiently waiting
Waiting to be recognized and appreciated the way it should be
How I can't understand why people can't see
How I've been waiting so patiently

JOSEPHINE DION CASEY

Smile

A smile is what brings the best out of you
It's something everybody should often do
A smile lights up your day
Each time you have something to say
A smile is what you should always have on your face
To show the happiness
The love and the peace
The love that is within
The happiness you sing
And the peace you share
To everyone that cares
Smile!
And show the joy and happiness it brings
Just smile

So Give A Little

It's not all about the money you know
But some people make it seem so
It's like the more money you make
The more you want to take
But why not be considerate and content with what you have
So give a little
It will put a smile on someone that's sad
A little makes a difference to someone with nothing
Because they will always see it as something
So give a little
Share a lot
And think of those that are more in need
Satisfy with what you have and do a good deed
In this moment and at this time
Be caring, kind and always of sound mind
So give a little
And comfort you may find

Some People Just Don't Appreciate Others

Some people just don't appreciate others
These people are all over even mothers
This is what I fail to see
Why and how can this be
Some people just don't appreciate hard work when they see it
They are so nonchalant and just let things sit
They don't seem to care or stop to think of others
I guess they see it's too much of a bother
But this is what some people need to see
They can't just let this be
So open your eyes today and see
How to really appreciate others

Feeling Alone

Here I am alone
Too embarrassed and scared
To pick up the phone
To call out for help
Instead of being by myself
Too ashamed and worried
Of what people might think
Too withdrawn to connect or link
So here I am alone
Too sad and weary I moan
Too distant and away I am
But all I need is a helping hand
To reach out and understand
To uplift me so I can change my tone
So I won't feel here all alone

JOSEPHINE DION CASEY

Reaching Out

I'm reaching out
With so much fear
So much doubt
But I have to be strong
Even if the wait is long
For they say good things comes
To those who wait
Yes I must believe this
And must have faith
And I pray to God each day
For I'm reaching out today
Someone will hear my cries
Someone will see these tears in my eyes
For I'm reaching out today
To someone to help me along the way

Beauty Is In The Eyes Of The Beholder

Beauty is in the eyes of the beholder
Beauty is in all of us even the soldier
Beauty is only skin deep
A pretty face some only want to keep
A beautiful mind
A heart that's kind
That is everlasting in time
For this is what the beholder may seek
Someone simple, someone meek
Beauty at its peak
Even when we age and get older
For beauty is in the eyes of the beholder

JOSEPHINE DION CASEY

Why Do I Feel Like This

Why do I feel like this
Is it because I'm sad
Is it because I'm mad
As I sit here writing this
And wonder about my list
List of things that are so wrong
That I can write down all day long
Why can't I get over this hurdle
That seems to be a never ending circle
But I must try and see the light
Try with all my strength and all my might
For one day I'll get over this feeling
And truly begin my healing

Jabok

I am me
What is it you see
Wanting me to be
Just another trouble maker
A forsaker
No I am me, Jabok
Yes I have dreadlocks
But why should this matter
I am here to praise God
As it is my heart's desire
For he is the one I admire
Jabok I say is my name
I may look lame
But I know God is surely glad I came
I am here in church to worship him
To give thanks to him
To ask him for direction
To show him affection
To guide me in every aspect of my life
In every section
Jabok I say is my name
God did not make us the same
We are all different
But are here for the same thing
To praise and worship him

JOSEPHINE DION CASEY

Show Me Love

Show me love
Show me grace
Show me your face
For I'm in love with you
And this is what I want you to do
Love me with all your heart
And I will never tear it apart
Show me love
Show me grace
Show me your face
Love me with all you've got
And I will surely love you a lot
Show me love
Show me grace
Show me your face
And your love will never go to waste

Give Me Peace

Give me peace
I need it today
I need it now this is what I say
Give me peace
To live my life
Give me peace
To go without strife
Give me peace to accept the present
Give me peace
God in heaven
Give me peace
This is what I need
In order to get ahead and succeed
Give me peace
This is what I ask the least
Give me peace

JOSEPHINE DION CASEY

Please Help Me God

Dear God please help me and guide me in the right way
Because I'm running out of options and what to say
Please help me God
To be courageous and strong
But how long do I wait God
How long
I need you now in each way possible
To show me through the path that seems impossible
Please help me God
For now is when I need you
To do what you do
Help me
Please help me God

Beautiful

Beautiful you are
In each way possible
See stars when I see you
Heart pounds
Full of joy
Full of sound
You are my everything
My captain
My right wing
So special to me
And will always be
Beautiful

Mixed Feelings

Don't you want to see me
Don't you want to feel me
Thought you said you love me
Thought you'd want to hug me
But where can you be
I don't know, I don't see
Will you come look for me
Show me you care for me
I don't know
And I don't like it so
Show me you care
Step out of fear
Do this I dare
Because
Don't you want to see me
Don't you want to feel me
Thought you said you love me
Thought you'd want to hug me

Never Heard

Will I be heard
I'm not absurd
Just want to be heard
Someone listen out there
Someone's got to hear
Don't judge me
Just be fair
Someone's got to care
I want to speak out loud
Speak in person, speak in a crowd
I just want to be heard

JOSEPHINE DION CASEY

Calm Cool Collected

Calm cool collected smooth
This is her, this is her mood
Walking down the street
You can hear the strides of her feet
Standing so at ease
Looking as a tease
Calm cool collected smooth
This is her, this is her mood
All put together
So sheik, all in leather
Hair slicked back in place
You can see her glorious face
Words flowing from her lips
As she drinks her tea in sips
Posture so firm and confident
She's a phene
So genuine, so serene
Calm cool collected smooth
This is her, this is her mood

Self-Worth

Longing to be loved again
Tired of just being your friend
Wanting to be held
To be cared about
To be shown affection
I don't need perfection
Longing for someone to treat me
Like a queen ought to be
But should this be the way I feel
Is this really a big deal
Should I look inside of me
To discover the real and see
Should I find love
Should I find hurt
I'm searching
But I need to find my self-worth

JOSEPHINE DION CASEY

Fake

You are fake
You are greedy
You become needy
It's like the more you make
The more you take
Why such a fake
A different face on the outside
One that you don't hide
For I see right through you
In what you do
Pretentious you are
But it won't get you far
Fake has its limit
It will eventually surface
So everyone can see
How a fake you can be

Dreaming

Free to dream
Free to live
Free to believe in what I do
Horizons and visions
Capture my mind
Inspiration is what I find
Looking for a better life
Without struggle, without strife
Finding the inspiration
While I look at these different aspects of life
Seizing the moment at its height
Dreaming of a better life
From a great view
A wondrous sight
Dreaming of a better life

JOSEPHINE DION CASEY

I Need You Lord To Be My Friend

So I'm here writing this
How to feel valued again
To be appreciated
To mean something
To gain confidence
To believe in myself again
I need you lord to be my friend
I've lost my self esteem
No longer proud or keen
I need to have faith
To hope for things never seen
I need to rise above this set back
Which has become an attack
I need to find my worth again
I need you lord to be my friend

I Know I Can

I can do it I know I can
All I need is God's helping hand
Just have to keep the faith and believe
That life is what we perceive
I will have hope
And stay calm and humble
Strong and firm, not to tumble
For I can do it I know I can
With God's help I will stand
Brave as I can ever be
Without fear you will see
For God will help me

JOSEPHINE DION CASEY

Empty Inside

Broken
Wounded
Empty inside
Lord please help me to ride this tide
The storms of life
Have surely brought strife
Lord help me, be on my side
Broken
Wounded
Empty inside
Lord help me, be my guide
Facing challenges throughout the day
Lord please help me, this is what I pray
It's never an easy road
And is often too much of a load
Broken
Wounded
Empty inside
Lord I call upon you
Please don't hide

Hope

Hope for all
Never should you fall
Never should you give up
Conquer all
Have hope, faith, trust and believe
For you will receive
All life's blessings
Learning everyday lessons
Believing that you will soar up high
Even with doubts and why's
Yes you should hail
Even if you fail
For there will always be hope for you to sail
In what you do and choose to pursue
It's an element in you
Hope

JOSEPHINE DION CASEY

A World So Wrong

Why do I live in a world so wrong
So wrong problems happen all day long
Why is this world so confused
So confused people don't know what to do
Why is it that this world has to have so much problems
So much problems you can't stand
Only if you wish you can
Why is it some people act so bad
When others are sad
This world that we live in is so wrong
I don't understand why everyday long
Why does it have to be this way
This way all night, all day
Why do things in this world have to be so hard to face
So complicated, so hard to understand
Why do wrong things go on everyday
Everyday in every way
In every way wrong as possible
Why is it this world is so wrong

Positive Thinking

Positive thinking gets you ahead
Surely true and well said
Positive thinking brings hope
Even in the tough times you'll cope
It will allow you to think
Outside the box
Think happy
Think good
And you'll overcome problems
The way you should
For positive thinking gets you ahead
It's surely true and well said

JOSEPHINE DION CASEY

What Love Is For Me

What love is for me
Is with someone who is meant to be
Someone who will bring me happiness
And fill my every dream
What love is for me
Is with someone special
Someone who will make me feel loved
Not pushed aside or shoved
What love is for me is like being cared about
Every minute, in every day
What love is for me
Is being loved by someone
Who would do anything for me
Would protect me
Would cherish me
Would love and care for me
What love is for me
Is like being someone special
Special to you forever
Special to you more than ever
That is what love is for me and
Everything I want you to be

Why Is Life This Way

Why do things have to happen this way
Happen all the time and everyday
Why does life have to be so hard
So hard to live with
So hard to face
Why does life has so much sorrow and pain
So much sorrow you cry
So much pain that you feel to die
Why is life so complicated
So complicated that you can't live with it
So complicated that you hate it
Why is it so much trouble and problems
Trouble you could never fix
Problems that will always seem to mix
Why does life have to be that way
Why

JOSEPHINE DION CASEY

Shine

Stand out
Give a shout
You are able
Remarkable and stable
Shine
Be the best you can be
Show it, let others see
Brilliant you are
To have come so far
So strong and bold
A secured hold
Shine
This is your time
Just shine

Why Are Roses Sweet To Me

Why are roses sweet to me
Is it a sign that we were meant to be
Is it a sign for eternity
Why is it every time I smell a rose
I start to think of you
Start thinking of your wonderful smile
That never goes away or hide
When I smell a rose
I remember the sweet smell you always had
And how you never made me sad
A rose to me is a symbol of love
Love that will last forever
Forever and ever
And never will that love go away
Not even for a day
Why are roses sweet to me
Because they remind me that we were meant to be

JOSEPHINE DION CASEY

Today I Feel Sad

Today I feel sad
Sad for what I had
Sad for what I could have had
Today I'm sad for many reasons
Reasons that hurt inside
Reasons that hurt outside
Today I feel the sadness
The sadness that's within me
The sadness that I cannot bare
The sadness that life's unfair
Today is the day I feel the unhappiness
The unhappiness in my heart
The unhappiness in my soul
Today is the day I feel sad

The Love Between Us

The love between us
Is more special than anything in this world
More special than anything
Even a diamond ring
Our love for each other
Is something that will go on forever
Go on as long as we live
As long as we still have each other to give
The love between us
Is something that will always be there
Something that will never go away
That is something I can always say
Each and everyday
For you and me are destined to be
And people can always see
The love that we share for each other
The passion we feel for one another
The trouble between us that doesn't even bother
For we are made for each other
And will always be together

JOSEPHINE DION CASEY

Give Thanks

Give thanks for everyday you live
Treat others right
Love, share and give
Give thanks for every breath you take
For some can't make it, some forsake
Give thanks for this very moment in time
Let this be a reminder on your mind
Give thanks for the simple things
Food, shelter, a door bell that rings
Give thanks for the journey you've taken
The distance, how far
For this is what has made you who you are
So give thanks for all you have

So Much Hatred

Why does there have to be so much hatred for one another
Just because we have a different race
We have different skin colours
We have a different face
Why do people hate each other because of this
Hate one another because we don't look the same
Hate each other because it's from a different place we came
Why does there have to be so much fighting
So much fighting that go on all day in this world
And sometimes people end up getting hurt
Hurt by someone saying something
Or hurt by someone fighting
Why can't people just accept people for who they are
It doesn't matter where you came from or how far
What matters is you treat others the way you would want to be treated
Equally with dignity
And most of all
With respect

JOSEPHINE DION CASEY

A Flower Filled With Love

A flower he gave me
Said that we were meant to be
A flower that has the sweetest smell
The prettiest colour and the tenderest touch
It's a flower filled with love I say
Which brings happiness to me each day
His flower looks as lovely as ever
Something that I'll cherish forever
His flower has captured
My heart
My soul
It's a flower to behold
A flower filled with love I say
His love that keeps me everyday
On that very day he told me
The flower is a symbol of our love
Our eternity
Our bond between us
His flower is something I will always keep
Because it's a flower filled with love I say

Do You Feel The Same

Do you feel the same as I do
Do you care for me
Then show me so I can see
Show me that you love me
Show me that we were meant to be
Do you even like me
The same way I like you
Is this what you like to do
Say you like me
When you know we aren't meant to be
Is this what you are doing
Hurting me
Hurting my heart
And tearing me apart
Do you really like me
Or is this a joke
A joke so you can use me
Use me and make me look like a fool
So you'll just look cool
So do you feel this way
If you do tell me this very day
Tell me

JOSEPHINE DION CASEY

Don't Judge

She looks at her with disgrace
She looks at her in her face
Why such hate
She's just another human being
With a purpose, a meaning
She judges her based on her appearance
Not looking beyond that
Not looking at the facts
Why judge her when she doesn't know
What she might reap or sow
Try switching places
Being in her shoe
She surely won't know what to do
Imagine being her for a day or two
She may not attain or subdue
So don't judge
She's just a person just like you

Undecided Feelings

Does she love him
Does he love her
Who knows what will occur
She has feelings for him
Sometimes a sudden whim
But will she go out on a limb
She is afraid at times
To take that chance
Not leaving any room for her heart to advance
She's cautious at times
Not leaving any signs
To show she cares about him
To show feelings she may love him
She's concerned he may not love her
But who knows what may occur

JOSEPHINE DION CASEY

Blessings For This New Life

Blessing for this new life
Open hearts to see right
Shower with love
Be kind
Peaceful as a dove
Bringing happiness to all
Knocking down broken walls
What a blessing you would be
He or she

Christmas Joy

Christmas joy
Filling the air
So much happiness
So much care
It's the Christmas cheer
In the atmosphere
That brings these happy emotions out of fear
Christmas joy
No need to be coy
It's the Christmas spirit
One with good merit
Delight, laughter, gladness bliss
One can never miss
This Christmas joy

JOSEPHINE DION CASEY

It's The Holiday Season

It's the holiday season
So smile
It goes without reason
Spending time with family
Kind gestures
Friendly faces
Sharing the love that embraces
This holiday season is one to hold memories
One to never forget
One that will always hold a mind set
So smile
It's the holiday season
It won't go without reason

Letting Go

Letting go of past situations
Letting go of hurt, pain, anger and shame
For there's no one to blame
Just let go and sustain
Release resentment and the pain
It's hard but you have to maintain
Stay calm and not vain
Reduce rage, tantrum and vexation
Embrace joy, peace, and happiness
Relax be calm and of good nature
Show pleasantness
Letting go is hard to do
If you don't it will consume you
Let go today
And no dismay
Take a deep breath
Free, liberate
Get in that mind state
You'll feel relieved, appeased and at ease
Let go

Reflection

Thoughts she thinks on
Observation she looks upon
Reproach and careful consideration
She sets into moderation
As she begins her reflection
No it wasn't a year of perfection
No it wasn't a year she showed affection
It was a year of trials and tribulation
It was a year of confusion
Towards the end she found God again
Someone to lean on
A dear friend
Towards the end
She found hope again
God has helped her to mend
Towards the end her faith had shown
It surely had grown
As she reflects on this year
She realizes God was always there
Waiting for her to find him
Waiting for her to recognize him
As she reflects on this year
She knows God was always near
To listen to her
Never letting her deter
As she reflects on this year
She acknowledges God will always be here
Now forever and evermore
This is her reflection

Edwards Brothers Malloy
Oxnard, CA USA
June 11, 2014